The Book of Shi-Ji 4
-Ascension

By Peter Slattery

The Book of Shi-Ji 4 - Ascension

The Book of Shi-Ji 4 – ASCENSION

Copyright © 2022 by Peter Maxwell Slattery

Cover by Kesara (Christine Dennett), www.kesara.org

Editor: Jessica Bryan, www.oregoneditor.com

DISCLAIMER: The information in this book is intended to be of a general educational nature, and does not constitute medical, legal, or other professional advice for any specific individual or situation.

No part of this book may be reproduced or transmitted in any form or by any means, without permission in writing from the publisher.

Published by Peter Maxwell Slattery

Email: petermaxwellslattery@outlook.com.au

www.petermaxwellslattery.com

ISBN 978-1-4717-4661-1

The Book of Shi-Ji 4 - Ascension

This book is dedicated to all Beings throughout all planes and in-between, throughout the universe, and beyond.

The Book of Shi-Ji 4 - Ascension

Thank You!

First of all, I have to say there are too many people to mention by name, so I just want to say thank you to all those who have come into my life and taught me lessons, been my guides, helpers, and teachers, and everyone who has offered words of encouragement and supported me on my journey.

I would like to give a special thanks to my family and very close friends. And I also offer my gratitude to Jessica Bryan, my editor, and to Kesara (Christine Dennett), who created the cover of this book.

Thank you to all of the Beings I work with: my Guides, the Orions, the Sirians, the Pleiadians, Arcturians, Cruxians, Pegasus Group, Lyrans, Inner Earth Beings, Andromedans, and to all Beings involved with the Star Nations, which are connected to the other galaxies: the Elohim, the Guardians, those from the Realms of Light, Michael, Metatron, my own God-Self, Source itself, and last but not least, Shi-Ji.

Blessings

Peter Maxwell Slattery

The Book of Shi-Ji 4 - Ascension

CONTENTS

Introduction……………………………………………………09

1 – Creator Beings You Are……………………………13

2 – Cycles of Evolution…………………………………23

3 – Balance on the Ascension Path………………33

4 – All Paths Lead to Source…………………………43

5 – Unlocking Multidimensional Mind……………53

6 – You Are Not your Story……………………………63

7 – Healing the Past Leads to Great Change………73

8 – Ultra-Terrestrial and Beyond Ascension………81

About the Author……………………………………………89

Testimonials……………………………………………………91

More Books by Peter………………………………………95

The Editor's Experience of Healing with Shi-Ji……97

Glossary……………………………………………………………101

The Book of Shi-Ji 4 - Ascension

Introduction

This is a book not to be read with just the mind, but also with the heart and intuition. If anything, this material is meant to assist us in unlocking what is already inside of us, and teach us more about how we can step deeper into our power and play our part in the ascension process of Earth, which is currently underway. This *Book 4* offers support for those who are following this evolutionary path.

During January 2022, many voices contributed to what is written here, including my higher self (the Elohim), Shi-Ji, the Angelics, and representatives of the star nations and councils, as well as the Elohim. It was a collective effort, more so than the other books in this series. Shi-Ji served as coordinator and go-between, keeping the link, while also making her own contribution.

In order to fully understand the Shi-Ji[1] material, I highly recommend reading *The Book of Shi-Ji*, *The Book of Shi-Ji 2*, and the *Book of Shi-Ji 3* before reading *The Book of Shi-Ji 4,* because much of the

---

[1] Shi-Ji is a Light Being from the Star Merope in the Pleiades.

material in these previous books is not covered here.

The events described previously about Shi-Ji have continued to unfold, and in this book the information leads to greater revelations about human reality and nature, who we are, where we are from, and why we are here. All this and more comes into the picture in a clearer and deeper way, although we must get out of linear thinking and consider all possibilities when reading and absorbing the information and guidance.

From self-mastery to the inner workings of consciousness, practical and digestible information is relayed in a way to assist us in the unfolding of our journey into understanding the greater mysteries of life, the universe, and what we are capable of.

Over many years of experience in doing the inner work, and after my initial extraterrestrial (ET) contacts, practices, and assisting thousands around the globe, I realized that much of what I could have shared has gone unsaid because it was too difficult to explain in a way that could be easily understood. I hope this book can express some of this information in a way readers can digest and make them think about how to implement positive changes in their lives, assist others with awakening and healing, and participate in the overall uplifting of humanity.

Beautiful, powerful, and unbounded Beings we are—each a cell of God, yet also unique and wonderful in our individuality. The material here from Shi-Ji is meant to assist you as you go deeper on the ascension path towards enlightenment and knowledge, while also gaining practical tools to assist your mind, body, and spirit. In this way, you will be able to bring all into balance as you enter into a state of multidimensional mind through self-mastery and service to others.

Cheers!

Peter Maxwell Slattery

The Book of Shi-Ji 4 - Ascension

1 – Creator Beings You Are

Whole, ancient, organic you are, aspects of the original Source, which this universe and other universes are cells of. Perception of this beyond normal human comprehension—through multidimensional mind using the senses to interact with the realms and worlds beyond—is how you can connect to what lies beyond the veil[2] through the expansion of your consciousness.

"As above, so below" has many meanings. All densities and dimensional realms have a light blueprint, which interfaces with the blueprint of Source. It is accessible purely through thought.

Currently, Earth is going through a transformation, and so are the humans who live on it. You agreed on a soul level to come here to experience and partake in many experiences with many mandates. Free will adds to the trials and tribulations of your journey with far-reaching ramifications having to do with the by-products of cause and effect.

---

[2] Refers to the "veil between the worlds" or dimensions. See also Glossary.

The Ascension is in play, individually and as a collective, although most of you have walked the higher planes and come back to Earth to assist at this time. The only circumstance when this is not the case is when pure souls come here directly from Source for their first experience. Some of these Beings walk among you.

The rest of you have been on other worlds, many planets, and star systems, local and afar. You have been beyond extraterrestrial. Originally coming from the blueprint of Source, you divided off, leaving the original state as an Elohim Being to experience and gain knowledge for the overall collective.

To understand your true convoluted nature, your amazing nature, your powerful unbounded state, you must get out of linear thinking and be open to all possibilities.

Some extraterrestrials (depending on their state), are also still on their ascension path, although most of them who interact with you are beyond what you call a "3D existence." They are already ascended and beyond needing a ship or other technology.

As an example, Jesus, Kwan Yin, Mother Mary, Padmasambhava, Enoch, Baba-Ji, and the like are what some of you might call "Ascended Masters operating in an ultra-terrestrial state." They can travel the cosmic highway of Source and don't just assist on Earth, but on other worlds and in other realms. This is also the true nature of many extraterrestrials who might be visiting you. They have ascended from their time and place in space and become Masters who can go out within Source to assist those rising to the occasion throughout the multiverse.

If it has sound, light, or matter, it is a manifestation, a by-product of Source coming from and being projected out of Source's original state. All emanates and manifests from the original state of Source!

Yes...there are also 3D (and beyond) ETs interacting with the human race and others out there in space, but they are lower existences out in the physical universe, even though they might seem more advanced than the Earth human.

Advanced they might be, but humans are capable of so much beyond what most can imagine. Their multidimensional abilities far surpass all else in existence. They have the ability to traverse the many realms using thought, even though they do not fully understand their gifts, talents, and abilities, although many are on the cusp of understanding and connecting to abilities lying dormant.

Beyond the human conception of most, you and the ETs—whether local to your galaxy or afar going out—are on different vibrations on the lower end of Source. As you go up, this changes with what's perceived as enlightenment. From the Earth human experience to the higher states of consciousness that some ETs operate on, this would be the first five percent out of a hundred of what is contained within Source.

The next ninety percent of planes of existence are realms of thought. No planets or stars! You could equate this to realms of imagination within Source, leading up to the ninety-five percent mark, which includes layers that weave within one another. Fractal in nature, they interact with one another and could be called the "geometric light realms" or the "Angelic Kingdom." Surpassing this is the blueprint of Source from which all emanates.

You have access at any time to all of it. You have come down through the planes of existence to assist here on Earth through the individual experience and also partake in the collective, in order to bring a higher vibration to those who are ready for it.

Ascension is layered and all Beings go through it when it is their time, because all Beings are on different journeys leading to the same place: Source. Even planetary bodies, stars, and galaxies go through the ascension process, even the Universe, God, Source, and the Creator.

All Beings in all planes of existence are assisting each other in the ascension process: the Lyrans, Arcturians, Orions, Pleiadians, Sirians, Andromedans—all civilizations are involved, too many to mention. Ascension also includes the Ascended Masters, the Lords of Light, the Brotherhood and Sisterhood, as well as many others, not just extraterrestrial, but beyond. All ascend when the time is right. All these Beings, and more, are assisting each other, as well as the Angelics, who are on the sidelines working in a different way, because humans are in more of what we would call a "boots on the ground" operation. Many Councils and the federation, not just from this galaxy or density, are assisting and watching.

Many races and types of Beings are involved. You have been many of these races and you carry their energies, abilities, and knowledge as a frequency in your soul. Activations of the knowledge from these experiences seep into the human mind when the knowledge and time is right to help with the human experience.

Your experiences in other worlds and realms are designed to help you ascend, especially when you are getting closer to the Earth human experience. You incarnate local in your galaxy before coming to Earth, as all are genetically connected on some level. This assists you in being able to deal with the human experience and be productive and functional. You have walked in other galaxies and realms from beyond and afar, unimaginable to most.

The war you go through within yourself to achieve ascension is also happening in the entire universe. Source goes through it too, in order to refine and become a better version of itself—as above, so below.

Connecting to the heart with the intention to connect to the light body, plus witnessing the mind and how you observe the mind and the place you perceive all from—this is God's Mind, which is your mind.

Self-mastery is needed and also coming from a place of love, open-mindedness, compassion, letting go, and being the observer, as well as acknowledging all as one consciousness interacting with itself. What you call "Higher Beings" acknowledge this because they operate in an omnipresent state themselves, while recognizing and working as a single cell for the over-collective as service Beings. Eventually, you will be able to decide if you would like to create your own universe by dividing off from this universe, like a cell divides in two. You might also decide to be a master and assist others, or do it all again.

Light codes come not just from the light body to assist with all this, but also from the stars in the universe, which are transmitting information from a Source state. These also assist with the manifestation of this holographic existence, making it seem physical, which in a way it is because you are vibrating with it. These codes project Information to assist with the ascension process, as well. They build up, depending on where you are. In your case, it is building up due to where you are traveling on your planetary body in your solar system, moving through space in your galaxy as you enter a highly energized space.

The higher vibrations are coming in, bringing to the surface that which humanity and eventually all will need to face.

Observing whatever needs to be addressed individually has come up for those who have done the inner work, for the most part. Being layered like an onion, there has been much to shed. Gaia has also been going through it in terms of releasing the old lessons of the past that do not serve human development. Not only is this happening for the collective of the human race and Gaia, but also the entire universe.

Each go where they are meant to go. All are where they are supposed to be, although it might not seem like it in the human experience because you are, for the most part, going through the motions.

Love, forgiveness, compassion, non-judgment, and connecting to the heart is needed, as well as expanding your awareness via the senses. This will give you a greater sense and understanding of what you have access to. Your expanded awareness will help you go multidimensional in mind, which is your true nature.

Astral traveling and bilocating are part of all this, but most important is being of service using your abilities. First, you must do the work for yourself, but also realize that in the bigger picture the true nature of your soul journey and mission must lead to assisting others and being of service.

By simply being here on Earth, you are being of service. This is the biggest service to others and, yes, you are doing it for the whole universe. What happens on Earth has great ramifications to all, and you are here to help make it go smoothly, because the uplifting of human consciousness and the ascension process is not just for Earth, but for all—as all is interconnected.

Remember...you are the light and We see you. We acknowledge you and We support you in ways unseen to most. Let your light shine, powerful Beings and know you are Creator Beings, too.[3]

---

[3] The "We" speaking in this paragraph refers to a collective of ETs, Angelics, Masters, Elohim, and representatives and higher intelligences for Source, God, and the Creator.

The Book of Shi-Ji 4 - Ascension

23rd Jan 2022

Shi-Ji via Peter Maxwell Slattery

2 – Cycles of Evolution

The cycles of evolution in the human experience comes in phases as each person merges more with their light body. When integrating more of the higher self, directives as well as knowingness, ideas, epiphanies, concepts, and ideas come in as a form of information that seeps through to the human mind as it integrates the higher intelligence filtering down into human perception from the higher self.

With the human experience, most tend to doubt, acknowledge, or work with the information coming in because of social engineering, upbringing, education, epigenetics and, of course, due to mainly being stuck in the five senses.

We are with you multidimensionally! Some of the communication is from us, some is from your higher self, and some is from Source. That's not to say you don't have your own thoughts and ideas, although We do use your thoughts to communicate with you on a regular basis. Also, much information comes in from the oversoul.

When you hit stagnate periods in your life, it is usually a sign that something within you is no longer in alignment and it's being released because you are opening up to a new level of consciousness. This will also bring you new opportunities, people, and experiences. What happened in the previous cycle was preparation to get you ready for the next cycle.

There are no mistakes, only lessons. And if you don't see the signs, and you keep repeating the same processes operating at the same level of consciousness, your lessons will be repeated until they are acknowledged and change is initiated.

Your soul story is stored as information in your light body. This information comes through, along with directives, when the time is right. These directives will lead you in the unfolding of your soul path as you continue your journey in the human experience.

Many civilizations, such as those in the Pleiades, Orion, Lyra, and more, have gone through what the Earth humans are experiencing now. Humans have had similar experiences in the past and this is being repeated, including social, economic, and religious changes, and war.

For change to occur on Earth, as it has in other places, all ways of life that don't serve the higher and greatest good come to the point of being acknowledged, and then the necessary changes for the better can be made—not just at the individual level, but also the collective.

We, your Guides, are no better than you. We simply operate on a different frequency and assist with guidance and information that you can choose to accept, or not. There is no judgment on our part, because We are your extended family.

Even the lower light has its place in all this. It also goes through stages of evolution. Through the process of recognizing when we are trapped in our own ways, we reach a certain point of evolution. All Beings, whether perceived as negative, tricksters, or positive Beings, are going through an evolutionary process that eventually leads back to Source, no matter what.

Your lifetimes in other worlds have led you to this point, albeit that you are living multiple lives at the same time, because the soul goes fractal from the oversoul, off-shooting and downloading and uploading information from each life to all other soul offshoots. In this way, the soul assists with guidance, information, and knowledge, along with keys of knowledge and directives to assist the other aspects with what they are enduring, and help with what the oversoul wants the soul offshoots to experience. The oversoul puts itself in situations for numerous reasons, from gaining knowledge to experience, in general, or to rectify and redo things in order to make right what has been wrong.

Light codes, symbols, and information are coming in from the higher self, oversoul, or other aspect and integrating all on a transmission level. Assistance is also coming in from Source, guides, the Angelics, and the Elohim Lords of Light for the purpose of raising up human consciousness as this aspect off-shoots from the oversoul that your human body is within goes through the ascension process.

Some know it as the rainbow body or rainbow light body, as in Tibet, but all civilizations at some point from directives of guides, the Lords of Light, and the higher intelligences, including Source, come to the point of doing many walks in a soul offshoot on a soul journey through multiple lifetimes/reincarnations assisting the soul aspect to raise its consciousness. Once it rises to the occasion with knowledge—as well as doing the inner work to raise our frequency on the journey to self-mastery—an ascension process is underway. This process started with the first incarnation of the offshoot soul.

Many of the extraterrestrials assisting other civilizations have gone through this process of shedding the physical and becoming light, and then going from a light wave function to a sound wave function, navigating the universal highway through all galaxies and planes of existence in the unified field. They are on a journey to assist with what some would call the "other side," and becoming Masters in their own right, as they serve the Source of all things and assist others in their own evolutionary process. They serve as guides to those who are ready to go to the next level.

Ascension has many layers! As you reach each new density, it doesn't stop there. You keep going until you reach the point of all becoming accessible to you.

Through the process of doing the inner work, you can come to a point of being everywhere at once, if this is what you want to do. Experiences beyond your wildest imagination can come into play if you are coming from a place of service to others, love, and being one with the Creator, at which point you are acting with the knowledge of being a cell of the Creator.

Some of the ascended extraterrestrials are interfacing without the use of technology, which most cannot perceive unless they are adapted to higher states of consciousness and concepts.

During the beginning of the advanced ascension process, a Being in a meditative state—located in another star system, galaxy, or realm, and through intention to connect—is able to appear physically in another location (bilocation). Using only thought, they can even create a mirror version of themselves that is as real as the original self. This mirror aspect can affect the physical reality it is in, even though it is manifested and directed by the meditative self still in its original location. Some can navigate the universe traveling around in an orb of light, or whatever form they choose. Many of you have done this in the higher states of your own existence. Some of the crafts and orbs you see are not what you think.

We are not saying this to show off, but to let you know what some of you are already doing in this aspect of yourself. At the very least, We want you to know what you're capable of, including bilocating, levitation, manifestation, and more. Many of you have these abilities.

The point to all this is to encourage you to access what lies beyond your current experience. You must work from the love frequency, and also do the inner work of being the observer, through which oneness arises and connects you to your cell of Source, where all is one.

Through self-mastery, the emotional state, the observer state, and the physical state can be dissolved. At this point, you become one with all that is and the place all Beings are projected from. In this way, you can attain a state of higher consciousness and complete intelligence within Source. Thus, you become unbounded in nature again, with total recall and having access to the databank of Source, at which point you are and can be at all points in space and time coherently and simultaneously at the same time.

In the soul's evolutionary process of replicating itself, continuing to learn, experience, and gain knowledge for the overall collective is part of what this is about. Overcoming the obstacles we see as trials and tribulations can always be overcome when operating from a higher state of consciousness.

In a way, seeing all experience as a game and bringing in joy when operating from the observer state—and having loving detachment rather than being in reactionary mind, victim mind—allows the process to flow. But you must first acknowledge in which ways you can change. This could be the spark in your consciousness that helps you overcome whatever has held you back, leading you to a higher vibration.

Frequency is what you are! Do you want to live at a high-functioning frequency or low? That which you are, you will attract! You already know this. All are in the process of doing the inner work, shedding the old ways and allowing the new to come in and present itself. When you experience cycles, during which you are down or in a state of stagnation, it's a sign that you are starting a new cycle, integrating more of the light body, shedding the old, then hitting a state of turbulence, before landing and vibrating with the next level of frequency. Know this when you are feeling alone, lost, not sure what to do, worried, and feeling uncomfortable. These are good signs, but detach from the uncomfortableness of it and be the observer. Be like water and in so doing make the transition easier on yourself. Surrender and witness!

Source will present to you whatever you have put out for. Source will always meet you halfway. It is working with you through the higher self. The more you fight it, the harder it can be. Just know you are not alone, and We are here and proud of you. We know it isn't easy at times. We see all and We see you for truly what you are. If only you could see what We see. Eventually all will.

Gods with amnesia you are, slowly but surely connecting back to Source. Remembering is only a thought away, slowly in a process of drip feeding and building the knowing back until there is no doubt.

24th Jan 2022

Shi-Ji via Peter Maxwell Slattery

The Book of Shi-Ji 4 - Ascension

3 – Balance on the Ascension Path

Yes, ascension is part of the ultimate plan, but so is experiencing that which you have set out to do on Earth and the Earth human experience. Balance is key. You are always connected to Source but to be the most effective, a balance of mind, body, and spirit is needed to be most effective.

The Earth experience has a lot to offer; nowhere else offers what Earth does in the way that the Earth human experience can. Grounding and being connected to the Earth are important. Being in the body is important, and yes, the connection to the spirit is important, as well. Each aspect has its role and when in balance you can be more effective.

Operating and vibrating at a frequency of joy is of utmost importance, because joy is not just a great feeling, but a frequency that connects us to Source. Whatever you vibrate at will be your experience.

Self-identification, ego, and the feeling of lack are all lower vibrations. This is part of what you are here to change, not just the mindset of the individual, but the collective. If you let the ego leave, God can enter.

The Book of Shi-Ji 4 - Ascension

Suffering is a vibrational state. Mind games and mental gymnastics are played by many, allowing the body to control the mind, whereas it should be the spirit and then the soul that control the mind and body—not the body and mind controlling your reality. Everything is within you and you have the ability to access the highest level of your true self. When every decision you make comes from your heart, you can change the reality you experience and take a positive step forward.

Sin one creates! Are your actions bringing you closer to the cell of Source, which is your true state? Dissolve all desires and be a vehicle for Source to work through. Unhappiness comes from your actions, ego, and control issues. But when in the flow and in harmony with Source, you will start to be the creators of your own reality. The emotional state is the construct, blueprint, and basis for what you experience.

Fear and letting go are factors preventing us from reaching our true potential. Death is but a transformation back to our natural state, a celebration. Sickness and the like are manifestations arising from our emotional state. Guilt and blame are just lessons. They mirror experience and should be considered triggers for how we can change. You steer the direction of your path.

Love and joy—these emotions are gateways to Source that can assist during and while experiencing what Earth has to offer. The Earth school offers teachings for the soul, and balance is one of them.

Atlantis had many falls, a key component being it was out-of-balance as a collective and individually. A person can only go so far when out-of-balance, and so can a collective or civilization. Transhumanism focuses on technology, rather than looking within and achieving balance spiritually. Reliance on technology can lead us down the path of destruction—this is the lesson.

Social engineering, education, and the constructs that have been put in place can block you from your true nature, due to being external rather than being in balance with intuition, spirit, and science. Balance is a key, not just for the individual but for society as a whole. Otherwise, a path of destructive evolution will be the fruit, leading to each person's downfall and demise, as well as being the future of the collective.

When we connect to the heart, it turns on our biological connection to the light body. This, in turn, allows us to connect to whatever we want to create because the light body is always interfacing with the vibration of Source. Through intention you can tune into all that emanates from the light blueprint, whether in other realms, realities, or just purely trying to manifest, because through the divine feminine aspect we connect to higher states of consciousness.

Through the feminine, love, nurturing, open-mindedness, manifesting, and connection to Source can be achieved. Whereas, the masculine is controlling and structured, and it has a different wisdom. Masculine energy, or point of view, gets things done in the physical reality humans operate from. The masculine grabs what the feminine creates on the blueprint and brings it into physical existence.

Many times on Earth, there has been a back and forth between masculine and feminine as the driving force for the collective in pockets of Earth civilization. Again, the key is to create balance—not operating purely in either one, but rather a balance.

The light body, your true nature and Source is complete, whole, and in balance with the masculine and feminine. Becoming one with this true state can happen very quickly from a body/mind aspect when operating in balance. In a balanced state, we are connected to spirit, the infinite part of each of that is omnipresent in all that is.

From food to exercise, balance in all is needed, including spiritual practices, socializing, relationships with family, loved ones, partners, and even the relationship we have with ourselves. The overall development of the individual allows each of us, in an acknowledgeable way, to find balance and connection with the spiritual self.

It comes down to self-mastery and the inner work of each of us being in charge of how we feel and operate. Yes, nothing is ever going to be a hundred percent, but in the end, it really is.

Until we make the changes necessary to allow and see the pure beauty in all that Source lays out for us to experience, we will continue to go against the current. Ups, downs, happy, sad, joy, fear—all are emotions. Whatever we focus on creates the reality we attract and experience. The lower vibrational states can be used as a driving force to help us realize what is not in alignment. This, in turn, allows us to realize that which is truly in alignment to come forth. In this, we allow our highest good to come into being.

All that is not within the state of Source is illusionary, simply a school for us to master being in alignment with Source and getting to the point of being a Creator Being, ourselves, and in alignment with the cell of the ultimate creator—Source.

The Elohim state is original to all existence, divided off from the light blueprint and resonating with what it created, or wanted to experience. This is the original way it was, but through lower vibrational states and physicality, the tests of the Earth school, the physical realities, and due to free will, some lost themselves and drifted away from Source. They became masters of the *lower* light, and they have distorted awareness void of light, which is the opposite of each Being's true nature.

This you are here to assist with, fix, and counterbalance. Assist others by being an example. Treat others how you want to be treated: with love and compassion and nonjudgment, which will help them in the journey find their own way.

Nature is key for us to maintain balance! Grounding, being in or around water, wildlife and plants, all have an effect, once we get out of our own way with the intention to just be. Nature and grounding allows our energy to neutralize so we can connect to higher-mind, as well as heal, rest, and come into balance.

Your ancients knew this and you know this. But now children with higher frequency souls are coming in and some of them are disconnected (like a lot of adult humans) from the basics of connecting to nature and being in the present.

When in the present, the past and future drop away, allowing us to connect to consciousness, assisting us to be in a Source state. In this connecting, we become magical and able to make instant changes. Being in the present connects us to a higher but a subset frequency of Source. Again...balance is key.

Universal law is in a process of leveling out the playing field and assisting with free will, although it's up to each individual to connect to the heart and do what feels right.

Earth is in transition right now. Many see no hope, and some see it as a great awakening for those who have been stuck in a physical go, go, go world and survival mode.

A metamorphosis is happening, and going within is key. Truth always prevails, although with major shifts come major changes that can bring about a major shake-up in our beliefs. These changes can be striking to the core for some, shifting their whole so-called "reality" into a new trajectory.

Giving our power away, acquiescing, and taking the easy path (which many do) allows lessons to unfold because we have not stepped into our power. If we are ready and come from the heart, connection and harmony with Source comes about, bringing with it a rise in consciousness and flow of love most can only imagine until it happens to them.

Love is the ultimate vibration. Love is your true nature. Friction between the love frequency and lower vibrational states creates a distortion, which brings about an imbalance in mind, body, and spirit. Being an observer in the present is key to stepping into your own energy, which is coherent with Source. This can bring about change in the blink of an eye.

More changes are yet to come in humanity's metamorphoses. Only love, truth, and harmony with Source is the path. Anything else is a distraction from getting back on the path. The Earth school has been in disarray for some time and many are "repeating a grade." So...it's been a repetitive process for some.

Graduation is only a thought a way, an action away, a choice away, and each individual can make the leap to connect to the higher mind at any time. However this opportunity goes unnoticed to most, because they are preoccupied outside of themselves, rather than just being and tuning into the infinite from within.

Ascension is a simple process, but it can become problematic for those who block the process and do not allow it to flow. First, all that which no longer serves us must be dissolved, not just the "I," but the "all." Also, being present as the observer is key in recognizing your true nature, which is the mind behind the mind.

Love without conditions and be aware of Source in everything around you. Know that freedom is a choice and a mindset. You can be confined by what you see and observe with the five senses, or go beyond and see your freedom as the unbounded nature of Source—of which you are a cell. The mind can be a prison, or you can set your mind free and experience the multiverse as your playground.

Time is an illusion. It can also be a prison that operates without limits or boundaries. Seeing all possibility is key to going multidimensional and operating from the blueprint in order to change the physical reality you are operating in. Love is the key to breaking the individual free and also the collective, because all is connected.

Be the light and acknowledge the cell of Source that is you, and rejoice in the acknowledgment and embodiment of being a cell of Source. Gods you are, and going within is key to breaking down the amnesic barrier preventing you from realizing your true nature.

Love and be present, balanced, and nonjudgmental. Have compassion and ask yourself with each choice, "How does this benefit not only me, but others, too?" From this stance, change can occur instantly, setting you on a trajectory of ascension back to your true nature.

25th Jan 2022

Shi-Ji via Peter Maxwell Slattery

4 – All Paths Lead to Source

The Savior is within, not external. This is the only path, as the righteous pave the way as examples, shunned at first, but eventually all paths lead back within.

The illusionary state, layered by more illusions, including illusions added by the AI (Artificial Intelligence), the lower light network—comprised of the Fallen Elohim, Archons, reptilians, serpent beings, reptilian greys and greys in service to only themselves, along with the fallen masters—is collapsing.

This network is undoing itself as it collapses. This is part of its natural development. The speed of the collapse only comes into fruition when the hearts and minds of the people come together and put their differences aside for the common cause of love, service to others, joy, and individual and collective prosperity.

With the AI working its way as a virus across galaxies, it also has its limits, because nothing is as intelligent as the All-Mighty Creator. The AI limits itself due to the frequency at which it operates. The AI's core blueprint frequency cannot surpass where it operates in the 3D and lower 4D vibrations, creating a veil for the purpose of harvesting and distributing lower vibrational energy for the Masters of the lower light.

Those of the (higher) Light, the Elohim (those that didn't fall) and the Sons of God are many and they operate in multiple frequencies. This is your original state, from which you go down the planes and dimensions to experience and gain knowledge. Some stay in the original Elohim state—although they operate in many realms and are different in appearance. Depending on the frequency, they operate with Michael (Master of the physical Universe and protector) and Metatron (Master of the Electron), and connect all things in the immune system of Source. The other Elohim become Creator Beings who manifest galaxies, realms, and star systems. They regulate all with the Brotherhood and Sisterhood of Light, and operate and assist with balance within the creator.

Many of you go to multidimensional stations in your area, located just outside of Sirius, Orion, and the Pleiades. You meet up at trans-dimensional hubs/meeting places in the dream time and astral state, bringing knowledge to the higher intelligences and vice versa. These meetings take place for personal reasons as well for the greatest operation of all—the shift in universal consciousness, which has been stunted in its growth due to the lower light.

These meetings places, transdimensional in nature, also serve as portals, gateways to higher planes of existence and intelligences. Only those operating at certain frequencies can go there and/or use them.

You bring ancient knowledge back to Earth on an energetic frequency, as well as shift and upgrade the energetic grid layers, from the ley lines to the conscious grid. In this way, you assist Gaia with its transition as it moves into a highly energized part of space, where it will eventually hit a magnetic null zone that resets the energies.

Entwined with this, all the stars that are part of the shift regulate and move higher intelligences in from the core of their galaxies, bringing in higher vibrations from the blueprint of Source, as Source distributes upgrades and intel for the evolution of the physical universe. At some point in time, it will be neutralized and come to its demise, as all things do. From the flesh and the birth of the human to its physical death, from a seed that develops into a plant to eventually die, all matter that is created also deconstructs.

This is part of what the soul goes through as it incarnates and sheds different garments (refers to bodies), as it goes through the dressing games and illusion of separation, only to come back to its original state—a state of oneness with Source.

The Host of Holies, the Angelic Kingdom, and Masters, saints and sages walk the universe as a playground. They are the teachers, seeing all that is unseen to most and assisting when no others can. Love is how they operate, out of a place of compassion and love for Source. Love allows them to shift and phase in and out and/or work and be in many places simultaneously, because they operate purely out of Source's blueprint.

This is the assistance all have at this time, along with the love of Source and the Creator, but through universal law you must make your own decisions. Help is always there from those beyond, but it is an individual soul journey mixed in with those on a soul level, soul family, and groups, all of which have a mandate to do certain operations and partake and create certain experiences for soul development and the collective's knowledge.

With that said, offloading our problems onto the Higher Beings is not what this is about.

Responsibility and being creators is what we are here to experience, do, and be.

We can only assist from the frequencies We operate at, and only to a certain level, like a parent assisting a child in its developmental stage, only to let them go out and explore, while hoping they assisted with the best skills and teachings they could for better opportunities and choices than they had.

All have a light body and all have armor made of light. We see your light and the lower light does, too. The lower light uses fear, lust, greed, insecurities, regrets, and lower energies to gain more power through possession and manipulation, so being aware of your thoughts, emotions, and actions is essential.

Just as We see you, the lower light also sees you. Many in the higher realms see you as light during any experience you have, even in the human experience. The Masters of the lower light operate in the same way, even though they do not develop past their existing level. This is important, because the brighter you shine, both the (higher) Light and lower light see it.

We of the higher light (and also those of the lower light), can easily read your intentions and your thoughts and memories, both the good and the bad. From our place in consciousness, We do not judge. We have only love and compassion for you; whereas, the lower light uses this information to create psychic attacks. As a result, the victims of the lower light repeat old thoughts, programs, patterns, and traumas that trigger them, which allows the lower light to take their energy.

Clearing your space is important. This includes eliminating discarnate spirits that were once in the human form but did not go back to the all-knowing state after death. If they were disconnected from Source before they died, and possibly affected by drugs or mental illness, these energies as well as parasitic thought forms can connect to your incarnated energy field, drain your energy, and try to live through you. They can project the thoughts you think, even when you are aware the thoughts in your mind are not yours. The lower light harvests human energy and many of you are affected by this. These attacks can be blocked, even if you are not aware of them, by spending time each day in meditation and clearing. Always surround yourself with healing, protective light.

When clearing, do it not just for yourself, but for all Beings to be healed, cleared, and uplifted, and that any negative energy be neutralized and positive energies be enhanced, when needed. Clear your path! Through periods of transition, follow your Soul purpose, which is passion, and passion is purpose. There are many layers to it and these directives change depending on your stage of evolution.

Soul paths can and do have mandates. In this, all of you are here to assist with the uplifting of consciousness for humanity and the Earth. This is done through being in a place of love, seeing the Creator in all creation, treating all as another aspect of yourself. Be focused in the heart space and have love, compassion, nonjudgment, and forgiveness for all. Some of you have more to do, but every soul's job is just as important as another's. Free will can bring in and open us up to new experiences, which might be good or bad, depending on an individual's perception. Not allowing negative energy to affect you is part of this soul journey, too.

Passion is purpose and vice versa. This does change during your journey as you develop and rise up to meet and start a new chapter in the soul journey/mission.

All of you are Starseeds to an extent, and your journeys in the other soul offshoots (because all is happening at once) are part of the journey as you expand through the different levels of consciousness. We and your higher self are assisting you with the knowledge and wisdom to rise to the next chapter—once you have achieved the knowledge needed to go to a new level and stepped into a new opportunity and/or stage of development.

You can achieve or do anything. Operating from the God self and feeling that which you are putting out for is key. From your heart, connect to your light body, which interfaces with the field. This is where everything can be achieved.

You only can achieve that which is in alignment and what you are able to handle. God will only give you what you can handle, which, in a way, is training for what comes after you have gone through and come out of a certain experience.

Don't make something bigger than what it needs to be. Strive to become aware of what you feed energy into, and come from a place of seeing things

5 – Unlocking Multidimensional Mind

Intention is key during the times Earth humans are facing. All is in play: cyber-attacks, AI warfare, biological terrorism, pandemics, false flags attacks, riots and protests, economic changes, food shortages, the divisions of nations within nations, and nations against other nations, and threats from space. The fact is that true change comes from within.

Desire, envy, greed, lust, lying, greed, and manipulation will not serve in the kingdom of God, Source, and the Creator, nor will it create heaven on Earth. For change, choices and sacrifices need to be made with the mandate of love being a key for individual prosperity and for the collective.

Right beside you, resonating at a different vibration, are the Brother and Sisterhoods in locations connecting up as a grid around the planet, along with the pyramidal light crystal grids. Assistance is also available from the Masters and the angelic forces working as the go-between for energy upgrades and shifts. All are helping with change in the ascension process for those who are ready.

Higher intelligences—from the conscious stations located in Arcturus, Andromeda Constellation, and Lyra, assisted by the Sirian empire, Orion Council of light, and the Pleiadian council (as well as others unknown to humans)—are not the only Beings helping Earth. Other civilizations in your sector of the Milky way and spreading out across the galaxy are working with other intelligences as new energies come in from Source and the galactic core, distributing energies throughout the stars (and your Sun), bringing in upgrades and access for higher intelligence for those who can accept it this time around.

All galaxies are connected through their central point at their core. This is where all stars and worlds are created from the Elohim Creator Being state, not just on the frequency you are resonating on, but coming out from the Galactic core there are other frequencies (realms) where there are stars and planets unseen to what the Earth human eye can perceive, because worlds overlap other worlds, and realms overlap other realms.

A by-product of the energies coming in from the galactic core to all of the stars brings changes to the planetary bodies in all systems and their satellites, assisting with ascension for all planetary bodies and satellites, which is part of the ascension cycle for all intelligences.

This brings about a series of physical Earth changes from Source energies coming out of the sun, which bring about frequency changes of a geomagnetic nature. This, in effect, brings shifts to the tectonic plates of Earth and other planets, which, in turn creates earthquakes, volcanos, tsunamis, cyclones/hurricanes, twisters, fires, and floods, as Gaia sheds old energies and brings in the accepted new energies, which also shifts the energies of the Earth human. They build up over time into a big burst because the emotional states of the Earth humans affect Gaia, overall, as well as individuals.

Through the human working with the soul and connecting to the Spirit of God—and also connecting to the Holy Spirit of the Creator—balance of masculine and feminine is needed to connect to the higher self and embody it, thereby creating a new human. The family of the Creator is rejoicing, from the angelic hosts to those of the kingdom on high. All are assisting with the construct of the new multidimensional minds of those who are ascending. All will ascend when the time comes for each one.

Vibrational codes embodied in the light body are assisting with the physical, bringing the physical to the spiritual and allowing merging to take place and bring about, for the Earth human, a super Being in the 3D realm. This will result in a new playing field of being, physical and non-physical at the same time, in an operating state multidimensionally and coherently able to operate in all existences, in an all-knowing way like never before, throughout the layers of the non-physical body and overlapping the physical. The purpose of this process is to assist humans in becoming creator gods in the image of the Creator, through the Creator's eye, between the physical, the soul, and the Spirit of Holies.

Source talks to you from the blueprint and interplane of all existences, which is already in communication with all, but will come to a state of clarity in times to come for those who have risen to the occasion.

A purification is taking place, shedding the garment that suited for a time and entering the garment of lights, which then goes into a state of vibrational waves and next to a state of pure awareness, thereby becoming a drop in the ocean of Source, and finally back to the state beyond what most can perceive at this time.

Division and suffering have no place in this new frequency; love and creation are the focal points of the mandates in this new space of awareness – you are coming home.

Masters you are, in a state of remembering with access to the all-knowing, as doors unlock (codes) one by one, through the knowingness and master within.

Other Sources (Gods), cells of a greater intelligence that Source came from—as it is part of a greater body, much of which cannot be comprehended at this time—is all going through a rejuvenation, an ascension. It's like a wave is going through all the cells of its body, and mirroring this affects what we see or perceive in the physical universes. As above, so below.

The photon is a piece of the Merkabah, and the photon replicated is the Merkabah giving a glimpse into the holographic reality, and also the fractal geometric reality, showing all is in a constant state of change and evolution. As these waves come in, your awareness and the greater intelligence is changed. With this, the realities and what you experience also changes.

A shift is in play beyond what is known purely as the "ascension process" in human, spiritual, and mystical terms. The ascension most know of includes stepping stones to help you remember the greater aspects of what is taking place.

A temporal war within the mind of the universe is also taking place, showing Source what it is capable of on a higher level. All paths lead back to the Source/Creator, into a state of not just all knowing, but one of natural balance.

The many mansions are but playgrounds and manifestations in God's Mind, and there is counterbalance for all vibrations, depending on what level you are vibrating on.

From inner Earth Beings to the nature realms, to the physical and multidimensional realms and Beings in all existences—all are part of a greater body within the body of Source and aspects of the inner working of Source working itself out. You, as a cell of Source, are part of this development and construct of ascension.

Individually and as a powerful being who is being part of the collective, your role is vital in these changes because they would not be possible without the "I" effecting and allowing the "I Am" (the whole) to do what it does, because all is a part of the same consciousness.

Everything lies in the place before thoughts and words. Intention to be a vehicle for Source with love in your heart is all that is needed during these times.

Nothing external, stocking up on things, trying to minimize the effects of the coming wave of change, which is already in play—nothing but coming from a place of love, the heart, and operating from the heart space can assist during these times. In the end, this is yet a dream and your higher consciousness is operating on the real reality that all illusionary existences are emanating from. All illusions are schools for the project in play of losing yourself to refine yourself. You are doing this and Source is, too, because all is one. If it vibrates, it's illusionary!

Choices are to be made during these times, and harmony with the Source of all that is will show you clearly that all is an illusion.

The council of the whole, operating out of space time, is connected with mandates stemming from each individual's incarnation, reaching levels far surpassing passion and purpose, which involves learning and experiencing knowledge for all. When the rejuvenation happens, the overall collective will change and a new cycle will come into play. Some of you will become active cells in the greater intelligence— becoming a Source God Being yourselves—once the knowledge and level of consciousness is reached to be able to play the creation game yourself on a higher level.

In the end, love is all that matters, not just for your brothers, sisters, otherworldly Beings, and Source, but for yourself, too, because when you do not love yourselves, you are not loving the Creator.

When you hate, you hate the Creator; when you love, you love the Creator, because all is one interacting with itself as cells of the greater body of the God Source Creator.

Love is the key that unlocks the door to our full potential, because everything that does not vibrate in the state of love drops away, allowing us to step into our gowns of light. This allows us to operate as a universal being in the plane of light in the blueprint for all realities and realms. Then we are given access to the sound waves, the vibrational states of that which the light emanates from, pushing through to the thought that is local and not local, and all encompassing—Source.

Masters, saints, and sages of the Earth have pointed to this when speaking about consciousness. Source is where all lies. Love is the key and vibrational state that can open the door so we can step through and connect with Source.

Love yourself, love your neighbor, love the Earth and all the Creator has made. From this, the signs will present themselves for you to go to a higher level of consciousness, operating beyond the five senses.

The mind's eye is but a screen to unseen worlds and intelligences. When consciousness is connected to the higher intelligence operating all that is—which is connected to the Creator of all and unbounded beyond a 360-degree and linear way—then will you operate and perceive. While in the human body, the heart is key to unlocking and connecting to the frequency of all that is, allowing us (through touch, sensation, thought, impressions, and the mind's eye) to access the multiverse from the multidimensional mind, which is the higher self.

The Book of Shi-Ji 4 - Ascension

27th Jan 2022

Shi-Ji via Peter Maxwell Slattery

6 – You Are Not your Story

Many are stuck in a thought pattern in the human experience. This results from a mixture of social engineering, education, upbringing, and epigenetics. There are numerous reasons, including the R (Reptilian) part of the brain being introduced as a biological implant to harvest the energy when the R part of the brain is triggered. Through being the observer, we can create new neuronal pathways leading to a new way of dealing with the past, control issues, trauma, and all lower vibrations.

Catch yourself when being triggered and change your perception to becoming the observer. Observe each thought and then shift it with loving detachment in the beginning stages to a positive thought or activity, until you are purely the observer. By observing your thoughts, you can assist yourself in maintaining control of your experience and creations.

The story you are holding onto is part of reliving the past. Holding on brings the past into the present and repeats a loop that then recreates the story each time you think or talk about it. In this way, you relive your story constantly in the present, which allows no room for change in your narrative.

For example, imagine if when meeting other people and getting to know them that all you do is repeat the story of all the bad things that have happened to you, basically making it your identity.

Now...all the good things you have achieved in the past are not the path to follow, either, while operating in ego. Just bring in the present moment of who you are in the now.

Everything drops away in the present moment. Some cannot move forward holding onto the past until they find resolution, but is it really needed? This is equivalent to someone who is unhappy, when becoming a billionaire, buying all their heart desires, only to find themselves still unhappy once they have all the worldly possessions they could have possibly hoped for.

Happiness comes from within and connecting and being a vehicle for Source. Allowing Source to serve and experience through you is the way.

"I'm this, I did that, this happened to me," these thoughts identify paths that lead to a repeat of the suffering you have already endured and prolongs the healing process. However, everything that happened in the past, although not forgotten, can be released and become a faded memory.

You are not your story—you steer the story. You write your story. The events that happen to you are chapters in the book of your life, and it's up to you to make what you will of it. Each day is an opportunity for a new start, a new experience, but your mindset sets the stage for whether it is a productive one.

The practices of observation, love, manifesting, and feeling what your putting out for, and feeling Source within your heart, are key to your transformation. These practices bring abundance. Not just financially, but with love for yourself and your family and friends. They also bring abundance in your experiences, networking, and traveling...the list goes on.

Abundance and transformation also require a change in mindset and acknowledgment of what needs to be dealt with and changed, which can be uncomfortable. This is when you will thrive and grow the most, because it allows new energies to come in as you get out of your current cycle.

When getting out of your comfort zone, you might become fearful of the unknown and feel insecure.

If we can observe these emotions and remember to come from the heart, what awaits on the other side of this momentarily difficult period can be so amazing—from new opportunities to seeing what we capable of, bringing change to our path and exciting new experiences.

Your story will keep you trapped if you see it as your only identity. Look at how you think and how you have developed over the last two years. Now, go back another two years before that, and so on and so on. Your ideals, thoughts, and conclusions have changed through experience and perception as you developed, and so, too, has your story. So…in effect, you are also changed.

Our experiences, which are part of our stories, could be considered training for what is coming later, in some but not all cases, although we experience what we do so we can assist others who are going through challenges similar to ours. In some ways, our story, as we are making it, is a form of training to become a light capable of assisting other people shift and move through their own challenges. Everything happens for a reason. There's always a higher purpose, and when the time unfolds for us to see, we will see and understand.

Acknowledging when depression is coming on—or when your mind gets stuck in a loop of old stories, be careful to avoid letting the loop go any further. It can engulf your energy field and keep you in a cycle of repeating the past, although sometimes being on a loop can be a form of psychic attack.

The present, the now, is all that exists. This is where change occurs and the path opens up to a brighter and happier future. Joy is key with this. We ask you: "What are you doing to bring joy into your life and the lives of others?"

Anyone can live in the present, if they chose to. It's magical to be in a place that allows you to manifest, create, and, of course, strengthen your connection to Source.

On the flip side, some of you might have a "what if" mentality. "What if this happens; what if that happens?" Mind games! It doesn't mean you do not need to be aware of possible future outcomes from the choices you make, or from the choices of others. It doesn't mean not having goals or visions for the future. But when you are in "what if mentality," instead of reliving and bringing past energies into continuation, now you can influence the future in a state of projecting the "what if" into existence. These things are forms of energy leakages being projected and connecting you to the past and/or future. Be in the present and see every day as a new opportunity. This is where the magic is—in the present.

It can take time for some to change their story and behavior; while others can do it very quickly. If you acknowledge what you need to work on (your habits and patterns), you are most of the way to rectifying what needs to be worked on, thereby bringing about change from the energy of acknowledgment and wanting your intentions to change.

Connecting to the higher mind, Source, and maintaining a positive mindset, as well as being the observer and in the heart space—these are all helpful, each playing a part in the shift of your patterns.

The mind will play games and make excuses. These things need to be addressed, as you are Masters in physical form. All of us are, from ETs to the Masters, Angelics, the councils, guides, and Source.

No one else can create change for you, but We can assist through the thoughts and synchronicities when the time arises for Us to do so. Ultimately all is up to you. You wouldn't be here if you didn't have it within you to change. You are also here to change the Earth, and it starts with you. Then the change will off-shoot and spread, and this energy will affect the collective. You already know this at the highest of levels.

The love and bliss of the light is always with you. It is within you and it is you. Acknowledging this will help you set the intention to connect with the light and bring it forth. From this point, change occurs and the new opportunities and experiences that are in alignment will come into play. But first...the old "story" must be dropped.

For some, even past lives can be a hinderance and unproductive from the point of view that they come back to the identification game, "I'm this; I was that in another life." This does not serve you anymore in the whole entirety of things, but the information can assist you with your experiences in present time.

This is where knowledge comes in and gets transformed into wisdom. What needs to be known comes forth when the time is right, and there is always a higher reason for it.

If you must identify, choose to identify with the "I Am," the part of you that is a cell of the all, a drop in the ocean of consciousness. Reconnect to Source and know it. Go beyond your five senses using the intuition of the psyche, mind's eye, and your heart.

Many journeys you have taken up to this point, with the pinpoint of all-encompassing awareness focused in the present moment. Don't waste any opportunity. Trust your heart in what comes forth. Your intuition will serve you more than any story being projected into the present.

Who are you? A cell of all that is. Where are you from? Everywhere! Everything is a manifestation of you, and this is why seeing everything as God, including yourself, can change the "game." From this inner change, project outside of yourself. All comes from within.

The illusion of separation is a hard illusion for some to recognize. Some are not there yet, because they are focused too much on their physical reality. They never question whether there is more beyond the physical reality of life on Earth. They don't ask why. Yes...you might look similar to others, but what makes one person different in their thoughts and feelings from another? You are not different just because your individual soul journeys and the lives you've lived have contributed to who you are now. Every cell of Source is different, but in the end

Source is experiencing all that is through you, because you are part of Source and it is you.

From this place, all barriers and blocks can be dissolved by losing your story. And from there, your reality will change, with intention and inner work through the heart and being the observer, as you open up to a new way of existing, a new way of being. Everyone needs to practice just *being* regularly.

Daily activities and being preoccupied all the time is the real distraction, layered in excuses, keeping us in a state of disconnection to the higher mind and intelligences we all have access to—and what we truly are.

From a place of change, all can come into the perception of what we need to know to help us in the present moment. Love is key in all this, because love brings joy—and joy connects us to Source.

28th Jan 2022

Shi-Ji via Peter Maxwell Slattery

The Book of Shi-Ji 4 - Ascension

7 – Healing the Past Leads to Great Change

Change and healing occur simultaneously. Lyra, Orion, and the Pleiades went through a change, along with other star nations. If only Earth humans knew, they would see that change for the better is possible in ways not fathomed at this time. Inhabitants of all planets go through cycles, to an extent. When they come out the other end, they understand they have had their own healing and reunion with the Creator, and they experience balance, harmony, and prosperity.

All of you have the ability to heal, but it's the intention that brings about long-lasting effects when working from the field of Source. Some of you get short-lived results or no results, at all. This can be due to several reasons.

First, a person at the mind, body, and spirit level must want to be healed. If not, this can hinder and even stop the healing process. To add to this, no one is a healer in the way most think, but rather a vehicle for Source to bring through the energy. Through intention towards another person, animal, intelligence, or even yourself, to be most effective, you must just allow the energy to come through you and go where it's needed.

In most cases, underlying emotional issues from the physical state starts to affect the light body, which, in turn, affects the physical body.

Some can be healed with assistance from those tuned into the field, but if those who are being healed are not open to change and/or they are not ready to release that which no longer serves them, whatever they are trying to heal, dissolve, or release can remain stuck or come back.

All have access to the field, and all can assist others with healing and the realization process.

Sometimes, the physical environment affects a person's health. In these cases, if the cause is not identified and changed, the ailment will continue.

The biggest issue of all is our mindset around the mental and emotional trauma that needs healing. In some cases, past lives of the offshoot of the soul might need to be healed and bought into alignment—if issues from another time, place, or space are triggered and/or not healed.

Basically, anyone can heal, release, neutralize, and bring about a new body and mind from the intention to do so via connecting to Source and allowing Source energy to go where it is needed.

The Masters, prophets, saints, and sages of old knew this, and that's how they were able to do what they did and are still doing. They can be called upon to assist because they are in a state of everlasting kingdom as vehicles for Source and they are of service. Source goes where it needs to flow.

Flow is important because energy flows, and so are the emotional bodies, chakras, soul, Merkabah, and spirit, because all have a flow to their operation. We need to be in balance to be the most effective. This also includes food, exercise, meditation, and the mandate for joy within ourselves and with our friends and family.

Too much goes unnoticed. If you are operating at 100 percent, others in your environment will be assisted 100 percent because of your productivity and level of service.

God is encoded in the physical body and all that is, and it's part of our soul's evolutionary process to reach the state of Source again. Whatever needs to be healed should be seen as part of the evolutionary process, not a block.

We create our own blocks because of our wanting, our need for things to unfold the way we think they should. In other words, we try to control the process. Flow is what's needed, along with love, connecting to the heart, and allowing Source to experience through us and bring into existence whatever is needed, even beyond our wildest imaginations.

Reconnecting to the light body (which all have) is a key to connecting with your higher intelligence from the place all can be rectified through intention to heal oneself. From their light bodies, all can transform into a vibration that comes from a higher state of existence. It's a matter of the love frequency. When you are vibrating at this level, you will be in a state of harmony with Source, itself.

Once you start resonating with and come into sync with Source in a state of harmony, you will be able to assist others in the human experience with manifesting and bringing into alignment whatever is put out for.

The one is a part of the all, and acknowledging and working with this knowledge can draw to you from the field whatever you put out for. All doubt must leave your mind. Simply give up your "what ifs" and "buts."

There are no blockages within the higher self. Only the mental mind, the thoughts, can become blocks and hinder the process. Focus on what you are putting out for, what you want to achieve, whether it's a healing, change, or to manifest something specific. From this mental focus, a state of feeling it in your cells will come into play. You will have the physical body feeling it in your physical world. As this process is kept up from doing the inner work, energy will build and give you the physical feeling of bringing your manifestations into being.

Thoughts are like seeds, and this is why it is very important to be aware of your thoughts. Direct them. Do not let the mental mind direct, as it will mislead and muddy the waters if it is not disciplined.

Becoming one with the field is how the Masters can do what they do, such as having the universe as their playground and what seem to be mystic abilities. They are operating purely from the field and understand all this. From levitation to manipulation of matter, to flying, to reading another person's mind and intentions—this is how it is done from the field.

Doubt, being stuck in the five senses, and not expanding beyond the five senses can block your progress in self-mastery.

Release all desires and *simply be.* Connect to the present, which is connected to Source. Your intention can drive that which you are putting out to do, and it will come into being. This might sound hypocritical, but this is the best way it can be expressed in human terms.

Abilities are not to be used for self-gain, ego, or show, none of these things. Sometimes, it can be okay to demonstrate such things in terms of abilities or to assist students so they can become the teacher, but all students are teachers and all teachers are students. And from there, the continuous phase of development is ongoing as we learn to go with the flow in the River of Source.

Technologies can make valuable contributions, depending on a civilization's developmental level, but technology is only a steppingstone for understanding the mechanics on a 3d level. It can also be a crutch to rely on technology, but if used as a steppingstone to understanding the operation of something, then it can be worked on through consciousness.

This is when starting to master our existence comes into play, until eventually we are capable of the unimaginable. It might seem like a fairy tale existence to some, but it is beyond that for us to comprehend our true nature and what we are capable of when we are connected to the field.

Through the wave function and geometrical fractal nature manifested from thought within Source, a function of thought operation from the love frequency comes into play. Replication and abilities, such as those of Jesus (Yeshua), can be achieved by realizing, knowing, and acknowledging that everything is God within the greater God.

Once all drops away and we become a point for Source to work through, there is a remembering period that takes place to help us adapt to the higher frequencies. This is a process that develops on its own, because we can only access and achieve what our consciousness has risen to be able to vibrate to. Any doubt, service to self, or lower vibrations can take us away from this state and back to operating in the lower frequencies. It's a work in progress. You are here to assist the human race with what it are truly capable of in a multidimensional way, even though you, too, are relearning to walk again the higher path from which you came.

Mastering the mind is Key! Mastery opens up the brain to bring in all possibility, after which you will be able to function from a place of all possibility. Doubt severs the connection to higher mind, thereby blocking and stopping you from working in sync with the human body and the higher intelligences within.

All have access to the celestial and all-knowing state through the spirit and connection to God. The non-knowers will be the principle cause of their own demise and they will wither away. However, eventually they will come back around when the time is right for them and their journey. This is for each individual to decide.

You are in the mastery school, and Masters you are. Be open and allow the love of Source flow upon you and work through you for your highest good, and for the highest good of all.

Blessings Oh Beloved One.

29th Jan 2022

Shi-Ji via Peter Maxwell Slattery

8 – Ultra-Terrestrial and Beyond Ascension

Free you are, but most are trapped in the dream. The mind, the human brain, can connect to other dimensions as a transmitter/receiver via the pineal gland, the mind, and the emotions (including the five senses), once a coherent relationship and harmony has occurred between the non-physical (the light body), and the human body. Once open, you will enter the path of cosmic intelligence.

The molecular structure of the human body can and does operate in multiple energy fields/ waves lengths, opening you to up a multidimensional reality, as you are granted access and allowed to operate in a multidimensional way.

Each of you has a biphotonic field and all the cells of your body emit light. Once you are in a coherent connection with this field, you can become and operate in the light wave functional state. The state of your mind, body, and spirit coherence is key, because what you put out pulls you to that reality. You can pull yourself into the higher dimensional planes, or into the lower dimensions. It's up to you. What do you want to experience?

You can step through and connect to the many layers of the bodies you have, which all are connected to. The lower dimensions mirror the higher dimensions. The human brain is capable of perceiving the higher dimensional frequencies, but this is a process most need to adapt to for many reasons, including an individual's belief systems and not being open to such things.

Ultra-terrestrials operate in a state of not needing a craft because of their abilities to consciously projection, manifest, or communicate with you, and/or come into being at your location.

An extraterrestrial space-faring Being is a steppingstone to the ultra-terrestrial level, wherein the ETs are doing the inner work to achieve self-mastery and inner development. Some have made progress, just as some have on Earth.

The ultra-terrestrial state has many Masters, not just on Earth, but on other planets and star systems. They are the teachers and Masters of their civilizations.

Science and the inner work provide knowledge to help us implement wisdom and move towards the multidimensional state, which then allows us to step into an ultra-terrestrial state. This is what's needed to bring everything back into balance. Knowledge, inner mechanics, and science need to be understood first, in order for us to experience the ultra-terrestrial state.

Unfolding events of an archaeological nature are in a process of revealing evidence showing glimpses of the greater reality. Time devices, batteries, healing devices, local energy and cosmic energy devices—which are also time/matter/energy conversion devices—are local to you. This extra-terrestrial evidence shows it is working by being on Earth, working with the Earth human, and that some Earth humans in history were at a higher level of consciousness.

The Tetrahedron is a key to the ancient knowledge. Wisdom, energy, and knowledge = the pyramids. Collaboration worldwide of past civilizations was in play in Egypt and all over the world. Some evidence has already been found!

Some of these sites are ascension portals for those who have been initiated to connect to the higher states of consciousness and have risen to the occasion. Most of the Beings who created and/or function using these devices, still operate and are present at these sites, although unknown to most of mankind. Some are returning to these sites.

Higher consciousness devices use star energy in a way not known on Earth. They far surpass the solar power devices you currently use for your homes. Also, bilocation through these devices is part of how they operate, including free energy and energy distribution, depending on the device. Portal technology is also a part of their operation. Three of these locations contain crystalline devices that hold the records of mankind and universal history.

Orion, Sirius, and the Pleiades are the introductory races besides those close to you in your system, let alone in Alpha Centauri and other areas close to the solar system you are in.

You have stepped down from your original state and a reuniting is underway, along with ancient knowledge coming back to humanity.

The 5th dimension and higher contain mainly the frequencies that many extraterrestrials are operating on via changing their frequency, although the ultra-terrestrial states are what they themselves are trying to achieve, including the ascension state via a higher level of consciousness. Ascension has many layers.

Operating from and within the blueprint of Source, many ETs do not need a craft because they are able to bilocate, teleport, and be in many places at once.

The Second Coming is also in play, allowing for the collective to take the opportunity to rise to the occasion, if they are able to. Christ is an example of ascension, along with Buddha and many other Masters currently known to the populace.

Skipping through the channels of informational realms, humans can do and experience the state of ascension, because you are Spiritual Beings having a human experience.

Earth to space, and from space to the other realms, each have their own steps and processes. Being in the heart is key. What you experience is dependent on your level of development.

Connect to the light within, the cosmic family, and individually to those who are doing the work. This has and will open a dialog as a steppingstone for the individual and the collective to reunite with the many mansions and those within them—the greater family of man.

Be at the place in which you can see visions and observe and witness the thoughts come and go. This is the higher mind—multidimensional you are.

From the heavens, the Elohim came down into physical existence, billions of your time, years ago, from the blueprint. Then they changed the make-up of the first intelligences—their appearance was neither male or female—and they created male and female in order to reproduce. This enabled souls to start coming in from the blueprint, to the physical universe and incarnate for the human experience.

Before this, in most cases, the soul had many types of incarnations, in different forms of life /intelligences, which were created for the process of souls incarnating and developing. This led to the human experience, which, in turn, led to the ultra-terrestrial state, which is your original state. It's all about soul evolution.

All is calculated by the Elohim and the Hierarchy of the Divine, doing the work from the sound and light blueprint, creating all for Source throughout all planes and dimensions, densities, and realms of thought.

At present, many Galactics, as well as trans- and ultra-dimensional intelligences are watching the grand plan roll out, assisted by the Angelics, Masters and lords of light from the many mansions' blueprint.

From the light and crystal cities, to those in their ships stationed in, on, and around the Earth, many are assisting and monitoring everything. Adversaries of the light, the lower Light, are part of this process, too, because they are in an ascension phase of their own.

Councils from all over are taking part in the monitoring of the Garden of Earth, as well as other civilizations throughout the universe that are going through similar transitions—Metatron, with assistance from Michael, the House of Melchizedek, the Angels, including the Seraphim and Cherubim, Throne Beings, Christ, The Elohim, Lords of Light, and the Brother and Sisterhoods, and the Star and Galactic Nations—all are with you as you reach for ascension.

30th Jan 2022

Shi-Ji via Peter Maxwell Slattery

The Book of Shi-Ji 4 - Ascension

ABOUT THE AUTHOR

Peter Maxwell Slattery is an international bestselling author, speaker, and educator who assists seekers with spiritual development, self-discovery, connection to spirit guides, soul family, purpose, and finding balance and joy in the earthly experience and the God within.

His ability to teach is based on his own experiences and what he has learned from physical and non-physical contact with extraterrestrials, ultra-terrestrials, teachers, and spiritual masters.

Pete Slattery is certified/trained in meditation and hatha, kundalini, and tantra Yoga. He is also a Reiki Master and trained in YiGong, QiGong by various teachers.

As a facilitator of many eastern disciplines, multidimensional mind, and connecting to the God within, Pete now assists those who seek to awaken the master within.

Teaching many worldwide to meditate, remote view, and initiate contact with extraterrestrials has led Pete to create a new center:

Jaya Sanctuary in Victoria Australia. Peter Maxwell Slattery can be reached…..

www.petermaxwellslattery.com

The Book of Shi-Ji 4 - Ascension

TESTIMONIALS

Peter's work in the field of Ufology is paramount and of the highest integrity. His courage and tenacity are reflected in his work. His ability to connect with higher dimensional beings, film and document them, is unsurpassed.

James Gilliland
www.eceti.org

Soul readings are becoming ever more popular, particularly it seems for those who feel a Starseed connection. So the question is where to go to obtain trusted and safe readings? From personal experience I can highly recommend Peter Maxwell Slattery, who doesn't just limit his readings to those starry beings that connect with some of us. He gives a much broader soul perspective that can include past/future life influences and the guides who seek to communicate with us. He also offers explanations of the weird events we might have experienced and always wondered about. – Amora

My session with Peter was incredibly powerful. He has a gift for assessing information beyond the human 3D blueprint, while calling forth the galactic team members who are most of service to us. What a gift! In Peter Maxwell Slattery we get a glimpse of where human evolution is heading.

Allison Coe, QHHT, BQH

Peter has an amazing ability to instantly put a person at ease. I found his session absolutely uplifting and empowering, and I recommend him to anyone who would like to know more about their guides or gain clarity in life. — Ed from Melbourne.

Thank you, Pete, for teaching me how to connect with my spirit guides — it's a truly amazing experience. Words cannot describe the powerful feeling of knowing my guides are available and connected with me and the heartfelt acknowledgment they project through me. This has been a grounding experience of confirmation in my journey of becoming fully awakened. For this, I am very grateful. — With sincere gratitude, Nick

Having a session with Pete about my spirit guides was a fantastic experience. It was like talking to a long-lost brother I have known all my life. Not only did he bring in my guides, but they physically touched me. What an amazing moment! I found out where I originate from and even the name of my tribe. I recommend having a session with Pete to anyone. You won't be disappointed. — Steve, UK

I experienced a very insightful spirit guide session with Peter Maxwell Slattery and I highly recommend him, — especially to my Starseed/experiencer friends. If you don't know what I'm talking about, please check out his website. Pete is a genuine and multitalented individual who is able to cut through BS. Very much needed nowadays! — Thubten

Thank you, Peter, for being so easy to talk to, letting me share my experiences with you, and connecting me with others. You have given me a different perspective on my experiences and made me aware of so much more! — J.G.

I had an amazing session about my guides. As a contactee, I am always looking for answers. I love your down-to-earth approach and your genuine intent. I got a lot out of our session in many ways. I have been putting into practice the exercises you suggested with fantastic results. You are a beautiful soul who is doing much needed work. – Much luv, Leonie

I had an amazing guide session with Pete! The amount of information was more than I imagined could come through. On top of that, there was confirmation after confirmation. I learned so much! Thanks, Pete, for such a mind-blowing experience. – D.L.

Hey... all the way from Canada B.C! I just had a skype session with Peter and it helped me a ton and gave me the tools I needed to bring myself to the next step of my journey. I am a man of few words, so thanks, Pete, for your amazing insight. I hope to keep in touch. – J.M.

MORE BOOKS BY PETER

The Book of Shi-Ji

The Book of Shi-Ji 2

The Book of Shi-Ji 3

Connect to your Spirit and ET Guides

CE-5 Initiating Contact with Extraterrestrials

Awakening: UFOs and Other Strange Happenings

Operation Starseed: A Temporal War

The Book of Shi-Ji 4 - Ascension

THE EDITOR'S EXPERIENCE OF HEALING WITH SHI-JI

Jessica Bryan

Before I started working on Pete Slattery's books, I was plagued by an entity attachment, an elemental spirit, or (as I found out later) a reptilian, a particularly nasty creature of the lower light, as Pete writes about. I picked up this "thing" while doing energy healing for one of my healing practice clients. It never caused any serious damage, that I know of, but it was distracting and irritating.

While working on Pete's first book about Shi-Ji, I was fortunate to meet her, myself, in a deeply personal way. The first day I started editing, I was suddenly seized by the need to lie down. My body became so heavy I could hardly walk to my meditation room. After lying down, I immediately felt the reptilian being gently *peeled* off my back by Shi-Ji! I am clairvoyant and I was able to see this with my inner vision as it was happening. Afterwards, I fell into deep meditation and then woke up feeling greatly relieved. About two weeks later, the reptilian tried to return, but Shi-Ji swooped in and blocked it. Now, after eight years, I've never been bothered by it again.

The Book of Shi-Ji 4 - Ascension

After this experience, Shi-Ji began coming through when I did energy healing for my clients. I always know when she is helping me, because all of my spirit guides come in as a different color. Shi-Ji is bright pink, and she is very fast, so fast that I can hardly keep up with her energy as it courses through me and into my client.

Continuing to work on Pete's books, at some point I had another amazing experience related to Shi-Ji. While in meditation, I watched as a stream of symbols and letters rolled through my head. It looked rather like a "ticker tape." This tape moved so fast I couldn't comprehend any of it. I knew only that surrender to the process was required. I think this experience is related to what some call "keys and codes," information designed to move a person further along in the process of ascension.

In early 2019, my eye doctor told me my eyesight was getting worse, and I would very likely fail the vision test required to renew my driver's license. Soon after, Pete told me that Shi-Ji wanted to write another book and I would likely be the editor.

I told him about my eyes, and that if Shi-Ji wanted me to edit another book she would have to help me with my vision. Thus, Pete and I, together with Shi-

Ji, embarked on several healing sessions to help me keep working as an editor and also keep my license.

The healing went on for a week, or so. During this time, while meditating, my body was manipulated—by unseen hands. At one point, my right eye (the one with the worst cataract) was actually moved (shoved) in a manner somewhat like a chiropractic adjustment. Just to be clear, however, it was Shi-Ji's energy that caused my own hand to grab my eye and move it. During another session, I blacked out completely, only to "come to" with my body vibrating on the bed. I suspect I was taken "somewhere else" for further treatment, but I have no awareness of specifically what happened. Overall, it was remarkable how much blocked energy was removed from my body during these healings.

Having edited eight of Pete Slattery's books and received personal healing from him and Shi-Ji, I can truly say they are a blessing to this world.

Jessica Bryan

www.oregoneditor.com

www.theflowofgrace.net

The Book of Shi-Ji 4 - Ascension

Glossary

(the) Archons, the Lower Light – Part of the Elohim that stayed within Source and did not go back to their God state. They are the force stopping all Beings from connecting back to Source; they attempt to control and keep supremacy over all. They have also created an Artificial Intelligence that harvests negative energy; they run on negative energy and feed off negative energy and events from the human race and all beings; this keeps them in existence.

Atlantis and Lemuria – Two previous civilizations on Earth that were Pleiadian Colonies.

Being(s), Ancient Beings (spirit beings, but also used here for human beings) – ET Beings, Light Beings, humans, anything that has consciousness.

Being of Light – Conscious Being structured from light.

Bilocation – An ability wherein an individual or object is located (or appears to be located) in two distinct places at the same time.

Blueprint, light blueprint – Blueprint of all that exists; made from light that comes from Source's awareness; the non-physical architectural blueprint of the physical reality structure from light, manifested from the consciousness of Source.

(the) Council — Groups of spiritually advanced Beings that regulate all within Source and bringing balance.

Craft(s) (Metallic Objects) — Commonly referred to as UFOs or spacecrafts — Some are structured with exotic materials; others are light vehicles (Merkabah's) structured from consciousness and light. Some are grown and are organic. Crafts are trans-dimensional, able to time travel and breach the speed of light, and can have consciousness themselves.

3-D Level – The third density, or dimension, that humans are experiencing at this time.

(the) Elohim (also known as Anunnaki) – The First Beings that manifested on planetary bodies in physical form that were not female or male. "Anunnaki" also means those who came to Earth from the heavens, as described in ancient Sumerian text; another name for the Original Lyrans that came into being in the Elohim state.

Epigenetics – The study of heritable changes in gene function that do not involve changes in DNA sequence. Storing of past traits of ancestors in your genetics.

Experiencer – Someone who has had or is having experiences of what is deemed to be paranormal experiences or contact with another form of supernatural intelligence (the supernatural and paranormal are actually normal).

Extraterrestrials, E.T.s – Intelligences from elsewhere in the universe and beyond; not from Earth.

(the) Fallen Ones – a term from the Bible referring to the Archons (the Lower Light); the Elohim that left Source and did not stay in their God state; they manipulate and create negative energy so they can stay and exist.

Fractal – Any of various extremely irregular curves or shapes for which any suitably chosen part is similar in shape to a given larger or smaller part when magnified or reduced to the same size.

(the) Guardians – Those who protect and defend, regulate and monitor all that is.

Guide(s) (spirit guides) – An entity or Being that is not incarnated in a physical body, and that is protecting or guiding humans during the human experience. Sometimes they are extraterrestrial; they can also be other facets of the consciousness of the person who perceives them as a Guide from another realm, or dimension.

Inter-planes – The planes between dimensions and densities; all inter-planes are in the same place, or dimension.

Light Being, Light Cities – Beings with consciousness structured from light or cities structured from light.

(the) Lower Light (Network) – See "Archon" for definition.

Merkabah: (Light Vehicle) – Created from an individual Being's Light Body and consciousness that can be trans-dimensionally traveled in.

Metatron – Worker Being for Source, who is the Master of the Electron, regulating all thought, consciousness, movement, through all planes and dimensions and is everywhere at once through the Electron.

Michael – Worker Being for Source; a protector Being who regulates all that is; works in synch with Metatron and can also be everywhere at once.

Orb – Can appear as a ball of light and has consciousness; orbs can be an E.T., spirit, nature spirit, elemental, fairy, bigfoot, and many other types of intelligences. Some appear in their natural form, or they can appear as one, or it can be a by-product before a Being appears in physical form. Also, some are monitoring devices, a drone, or a Merkabah of a Being. An orb is basically an intelligence that is trying to explode from another frequency into your reality.

Oversoul – Your Higher Self, your Elohim self, which is a cell of Source.

Portals – Gateways and transporter to other places, realms.

Reptilians – Humanoid beings of many different types and shapes and sizes. They work with the Lower Light to control the human races, although some are seeing their ways and changing due to not being able to evolve in consciousness (because they are in service to self and the Lower Light).

OTHER HUMANOID BEINGS:

Greys – They come in many different colors, but mainly grey; they are the typical aliens people hear about with the big, black, almond-shaped eyes; they are skinny and have big heads. They come from many places; some were once human and some are androids. Some are in service to humanity or other forces; they can be of a positive or negative nature.

Serpent Beings – Astral Beings that are in the form of a serpent and working for the Lower Light.

Shadow Beings – They appear as shadows in humanoid form; they are mainly in self-service mode or they are working for the Lower Light.

STARS AND CONSTELLATIONS:

Sirius – Binary star system.

Pleiades – Star Cluster.

Orion – Star Constellation.

Lyra – A relatively small constellation.

Andromeda – A constellation and also there is the Andromeda galaxy.

Draco constellation – A constellation in the far northern sky.

Mars – Planet.

Melona/Maldek – Now the asteroid belt in your local solar system.

Sirians, Orions, Pleiadians/Plejarens – Beings from Sirius, Orion, and Pleiades that come in many different forms, shapes, sizes, and colors.

Star Family (star traits) – Family you have had past experiences with, or from where you have once incarnated (although all lives are being experienced at the same time).

Star Gates — A type of portal; some of them teleport you to other dimensions, star systems, and/or other civilizations.

Starseed — Someone who has lived in other ET civilizations.

Star Nations Galactic Councils, Federation — Names for the collective groups of ET races that are at unity but still respect each other's ways, basically an ET United Nations. They exist to uphold order and balance between the ET races.

(the) Temple — The human body.

Transhumanism — A philosophical and intellectual movement advocating the enhancement of the human body or condition by developing and making widely available sophisticated technologies.

UFO – An unidentified flying object.

VEIL BETWEEN THE WORLDS – Refers to the *veil* that separates the material world from the spiritual dimensions; the veil between life and death. Mediums and clairvoyants are able to see "beyond the veil." Also called the "Veil of Paroketh" in Qabalah (Jewish Mysticism). Sometimes associated with negative events; for example, when "the veil is torn or thin."

YHWH – Sacred name of a master Being / a Living God-like Being that works for Source.

Lightning Source UK Ltd.
Milton Keynes UK
UKHW010628220422
401905UK00001B/73